Digital Detox: Reclaiming Your Life from the Screen

Break Free from the Hold of Your Devices in Weeks with Sustainable, Feel-good Strategies

Copyright © 2024 by L. Poore

All rights reserved.

No portion of this book may be reproduced in any form without written permission from the publisher or author, except as permitted by U.S. copyright law.

This publication is designed to provide accurate and authoritative information in regard to the subject matter covered. It is sold with the understanding that neither the author nor the publisher is engaged in rendering legal, investment, accounting or other professional services. While the publisher and author have used their best efforts in preparing this book, they make no representations or warranties with respect to the accuracy or completeness of the contents of this book and specifically disclaim any implied warranties of merchantability or fitness for a particular purpose. No warranty may be created or extended by sales representatives or written sales materials. The advice and strategies contained herein may not be suitable for your situation. You should consult with a professional when appropriate. Neither the publisher nor the author shall be liable for any loss of profit or any other commercial damages, including but not limited to special, incidental, consequential, personal, or other damages.

First edition 2024

Digital Detox: Reclaiming Your Life from the Screen 1

   Break Free from the Hold of Your Devices in Weeks with Sustainable, Feel-good Strategies 1

Preface 5

Chapter 1: From Convenience to Compulsion 7

   When Convenience Morphs into Compulsion 8

Chapter 2: Beyond Backaches: The Hidden Health Costs 17

   Is Your Smartphone Undermining Your Health? 19

Chapter 3: The High Price of Lost Time 25

   Is Your Screen Stealing Your Life's True Joy? 27

   Analyzing the Competition Between Device Usage and Personal Growth 28

   Reflecting on Missed Opportunities 29

   Practical Repurposing of Screen Time 30

Chapter 4: Captive to Connectivity: Battling FOMO 33

   Are You Truly Free If Your Phone Controls Your Emotions? 35

Chapter 5: Reboot Your Relationships: The Power of Digital Detox .. 43

   Is Your Digital Life Costing You Real Connections? 45

   The REBOOT Framework: A Descriptive Model for Digital Detox .. 49

Chapter 6: Discipline Through Scheduled Screen Time 53

   The Power of Scheduled Screen Time 55

Chapter 7: Creating Tech-Free Sanctuaries 63

Where Will Your Mind Wander Without Wi-Fi? 65

Chapter 8: Mindful Interaction with Technology 73

Harnessing Mindfulness to Master Your Digital Realm 75

Analytical Framework for Mindful Technology Use 80

Chapter 9: Replacing Pixels with Purpose 83

From Pixels to Purpose: Crafting a Healthier Reality 85

Chapter 10: Gradual Change for Lasting Success 93

From Incremental Changes to Profound Transformation 95

Epilogue 103

References 105

Preface

"We are drowning in information, while starving for wisdom." - E.O. Wilson

The wisdom to disconnect is a rare commodity in a world brimming with digital distractions. This book, *Digital Detox: Reclaiming Your Life from the Screen*, emerges as a beacon for those who feel tethered to their devices, providing a path to regain control and enrich their lives beyond the Screen.

The essence of this book revolves around the intricate dance between staying connected and nurturing our well-being. It tackles the pervasive issue of digital overconsumption, which hampers our physical, mental, and social health. Through a blend of research-backed strategies and heartfelt advice, it guides you on how to effectively manage your screen time, fostering a balanced life that values presence over pixels.

I was motivated to write this book after witnessing the struggles faced by many, myself included, and those around me. Friends lamented over lost family time due to evenings spent scrolling through feeds, while colleagues reported burnout from the relentless barrage of emails and notifications. Their experiences resonated deeply, mirroring a societal shift where online presence often overshadows real-world interactions.

Innovators advocating for tech-life balance, wellness experts emphasizing the repercussions of digital fatigue, and personal stories shared in casual conversations underscoring the need for change inspired me to embark on this journey. These interactions were instrumental in shaping the narrative and solutions presented in this book.

This book is especially for you if you've ever felt overwhelmed by your digital devices or if the fear of missing out keeps you endlessly online, yet you yearn for a more fulfilling offline life. There are no prerequisites besides an open mind and the willingness to try new approaches to old habits.

Considering the numerous options available, I appreciate your decision to engage with this book and value your time and investment. By the final pages, I hope you will gain insight and practical tools to empower you to embrace a healthier, more balanced lifestyle.

Thank you for embarking on this journey toward reclaiming your life from the Screen. As you turn these pages, may you find both inspiration and practical advice that resonate with your circumstances, encouraging a fruitful digital detox that restores your well-being and enriches your connections with the world.

Chapter 1: From Convenience to Compulsion

When Convenience Breeds Compulsion

His coffee steamed beside him, untouched and slowly blending with the cool air of his unheated apartment. His eyes, however, were not on the day breaking beyond his window but fixed upon the glaring screen of his smartphone. His fingers twitched involuntarily with each notification—a reflex honed by years of digital beckoning.

As he scrolled through endless notifications, Michael's mind wandered back to a simpler time when days began with sunlight rather than screen light. He remembered fishing trips with his father, where the only sounds were the lapping waves and their muted conversations. No pings interrupted their discussions, and no updates distracted their attention from the task. The contrast gnawed at him now as he swiped through emails.

The phone buzzed, snapping him back from his reverie to an urgent message from work. It was just past six in the morning, yet there was a crisis that couldn't wait—an irony not lost on Michael as he pondered how these devices that promised freedom had subtly forged chains of instant availability and constant alertness.

> He stood up and walked over to the window, pressing a palm against the cool glass. Outside, life was stirring gently into motion; inside, he felt trapped in a cycle of responsiveness that dulled more than just mornings but seeped into evenings and weekends, too.
>
> Michael's thoughts drifted to his niece, Emma, who would visit later today. She was growing up in a world where digital devices were even more intertwined with daily life than during his childhood. His heart sank as he considered her future—would she ever know peace away from digital demands? Or would she adapt differently, perhaps better?
>
> As he turned back from the window, resolving to limit his screen time today for Emma's sake, if not for his sanity, a question lingered: How much are we sacrificing for convenience?

When Convenience Morphs into Compulsion

The digital age promises unparalleled access to information and connectivity. However, as we stand amidst a plethora of digital devices, it becomes imperative to ask: at what point does convenience turn into compulsion? This chapter seeks to unpack the subtle yet profound journey from using technology as a practical tool to finding ourselves tethered to it, almost dependent on its presence. We begin by exploring how habitual interactions with digital devices have gradually rewired our behavioral patterns and psychological states, fostering a compulsive need to remain digitally connected.

The Evolution of Digital Dependency

Initially, technology served as a bridge to efficiency, reducing gaps in communication while enhancing our ability to access and process information swiftly. Yet, this utility has been double-edged. The constant availability of digital devices has subtly shifted their role from mere facilitators to becoming central to our daily routines. This shift is not just behavioral but deeply psychological—the ping of a notification often triggers an immediate, almost Pavlovian response to reach for one's phone.

Psychological Shifts: From Alertness to Anxiety

Understanding the psychological transformations that accompany prolonged device usage is crucial. Our brains, primed for alertness due to the evolutionary need to respond to threats, now misinterpret the constant stream of digital alerts as mini emergencies we must attend to. This state of heightened alertness was once reserved for genuine crises but is now triggered by every buzz and beep of our devices, leading to increased stress levels and anxiety over time.

Recognizing Signs of Compulsion

Another focal area of this discussion is identifying personal habits that signify a shift towards technological compulsion. Do you check your phone the first thing in the morning? Is your screen time increasing while your physical activity decreases? These behaviors indicate that convenience is veering into compulsion territory. Recognizing these signs early can help address them before they crystallize into more severe dependencies.

Balancing Digital and Real-Life Interactions

This book addresses these challenges by identifying the problem and providing actionable strategies designed to mitigate the impact of excessive screen time on our well-being. By effectively balancing digital interactions with real-life engagements, you will be equipped with knowledge and practical tools that foster healthier lifestyle choices.

Reclaiming Control Over Digital Habits

As we delve deeper into understanding our relationship with technology, it becomes apparent that reclaiming control is both necessary and possible. To do this, we must set conscious boundaries around device usage and understand the triggers that lead us back into compulsive behaviors. A balanced digital lifestyle is achievable through sustained effort and the right strategies.

By understanding these dynamics, this chapter sets the foundation for exploring how individuals can break free from the compulsive loops fostered by modern technology and instead use these powerful tools to enhance personal productivity and well-being. Recognizing and addressing our digital habits opens doors to improved mental and physical health and enriched personal relationships —reconnecting with ourselves and the tangible world in meaningful ways.

Understanding the Shift from Utility to Dependency

Technology began as a tool designed to enhance productivity and simplify daily routines. From the invention of the wheel to the creation of the Internet, each technological advance has been aimed at solving specific problems and increasing efficiency. Today, our digital devices continue this trend, offering endless communication, knowledge, and entertainment possibilities. However, the role of these devices has subtly shifted from being helpful tools to becoming essential components of our daily lives.

Imagine a world where every tool you use whispers your name, enticing you to pick it up and promising endless rewards. This is not a fantasy world but the reality of modern smartphones and digital devices. They beckon with notifications and alerts, creating a compelling need to engage. The accessibility of these devices means they are always within arm's reach, making it all too easy to move from using technology purposefully to compulsively checking it.

This compulsive behavior is not merely a bad habit; it indicates a more profound change in how we interact with our environment. Initially, digital devices saved time by speeding up tasks like communication and information gathering. Now, they consume time, with the average person spending several hours daily on their phone. This shift from saving to consuming time reflects a significant transformation in our relationship with technology.

The implications of this shift are profound. As we spend more time with our devices, we dedicate less time to face-to-face interactions, physical activities, and sleep. This change in behavior patterns points to a less pronounced dependency in the early days of digital technology.

Understanding this transition from utility to dependency is crucial for anyone looking to balance their digital and real-world lives.

Psychological Impacts of Compulsive Device Use

Studies have shown that excessive use of digital devices can lead to changes in the brain similar to those caused by substance addiction. These changes can affect areas of the brain responsible for attention, decision-making, and self-control. As digital interactions become a compulsive behavior, the brain begins associating the devices with pleasure and necessity, reinforcing the compulsion.

The allure of instant gratification from digital devices is akin to the siren's song—irresistible and potentially hazardous. Each ping could be a message, a like, or an update, pulling us back repeatedly. This continuous loop of notification and response has conditioned us to remain in a state of alertness, akin to Pavlov's dogs, who learned to associate a bell with receiving food.

This heightened alertness was once a survival mechanism valuable in situations requiring immediate action. However, in modern life, this constant state of readiness can lead to anxiety and stress. Our bodies are not designed for prolonged periods of psychological arousal, yet that is precisely what the compulsive use of digital devices promotes.

The psychological shift from using technology as a tool to experiencing anxiety when separated from our devices is a profound change. It transforms how we perceive and interact with the world, making it harder to disengage from the digital world and fully engage with the real one.

Identifying Signs of Technological Compulsion

Recognizing the signs of technological compulsion in ourselves can be challenging, as these behaviors have become normalized in our digital society. However, certain habits can indicate a shift toward dependency. For example, checking your phone first thing in the morning and last thing at night, feeling anxious when separated from your device, and spending more time online than intended all suggest a compulsive relationship with technology.

To explore this further, consider the analogy of a gardener who becomes so obsessed with watering his plants that he does it several times a day, regardless of whether the plants need water. This compulsive behavior disrupts his daily routine and harms the plants he aims to nurture. Similarly, our obsessive use of digital devices can disrupt our lives and degrade our well-being.

By understanding the transition from using technology as a tool to becoming dependent on it, recognizing the psychological changes associated with compulsive device use, and identifying personal habits indicative of this shift, we can begin to reclaim control over our digital lives.

The journey from using technology as a mere convenience to recognizing its role as a potential compulsion is critical for anyone looking to maintain a healthy digital lifestyle. This chapter has laid the groundwork by exploring how our interactions with digital devices have evolved. For many, what began as a tool to enhance productivity and connectivity has morphed into a source of constant psychological engagement. **Understanding this transition** is not just about acknowledging the existence of technology in our lives but recognizing how deeply it influences our daily behaviors and mental health.

Through exploring psychological changes, we've seen how continuous exposure to screens can alter our cognitive functions and emotional responses. This shift towards a state of perpetual alertness, meant only for emergencies, is now triggered by every ping and buzz of our devices. Recognizing these **psychological changes** is paramount as it helps us identify technology's subtle yet profound impact on our minds.

The most actionable insight is identifying personal habits that lean towards compulsion rather than convenience. By **acknowledging these habits**, individuals are better equipped to implement practical strategies that curb excessive screen time. Awareness is the first step towards change, and understanding one's patterns is crucial in setting realistic and practical boundaries with technology.

As we progress in this book, each chapter will build on these foundations, offering insights and practical solutions to help you reclaim control over your digital interactions. The strategies discussed will enhance your awareness and empower you to make informed choices about when and how you engage with technology.

The benefits of reading this book extend beyond acquiring knowledge; they involve fundamental, tangible changes in daily life that foster healthier relationships with our screens. By committing to this journey, you are setting the stage for a more balanced, productive, and mentally satisfying life away from the compulsive pull of digital devices.

Stay tuned for empowering strategies to guide you through a successful digital detox, ensuring that technology remains a tool that enriches your life rather than dominating it. Embrace this opportunity to transform your digital habits and discover the freedom that comes with a balanced approach to technology.

Chapter 2: Beyond Backaches: The Hidden Health Costs

How Far Can We Go Before We Must Retreat?

In the dim glow of the early evening, Tom sat by the window of his small but orderly kitchen, a glass of lukewarm tea forgotten at his side. Outside, the city hummed with rush hour's distant yet relentless energy. His gaze, however, remained fixed on the sleek smartphone lying ominously silent on the wooden table. It was an inanimate accuser, a reminder of his growing dependency that nudged him gently into isolation from more tangible realities.

Tom's mind wandered to last night's restless slumber—a mosaic of vivid dreams and abrupt awakenings. The blue light from endless screen time had seeped deeply into his circadian rhythms, disrupting them with the subtlety of a persistent drip eroding a sturdy rock. He remembered reading somewhere that such disruptions were associated with sleep problems and more severe health issues over time. His hand twitched involuntarily towards the phone, a conditioned response from hours of scrolling through endless feeds.

The room around him was quiet, except for the occasional clink of a neighbor's dishes or the distant bark of a dog—sounds that seemed to come from another world where people still engaged directly with life's textures. His chair creaked as he shifted, pulling himself away from those thoughts and back to his present reality. The walls, adorned with pictures from healthier days—hiking trips and beach outings—whispered tales of a life once lived fully.

The peaceful moment was abruptly interrupted by the loud cry of his niece from the living room —she was staying over while her parents were out of town. "Uncle Tom! Look what I drew!" Her voice pulled him like an anchor back to shore. As he entered the room and bent down to admire her crayon creation—a colorful depiction of their last trip to the park—he felt an ache for simpler times when joy wasn't mediated through pixels.

He listened attentively as she explained each stroke with earnest simplicity. Here was life in its purest form, unfiltered and vibrant. Yet, he couldn't shake off how these moments were often captured through lenses and screens, preserved not in memory but in digital albums.

As he tucked her into bed later that evening under a canopy of glow-in-the-dark stars stuck to her ceiling—an artificial mimicry of nature's vastness—he wondered about balance. How could one navigate this modern labyrinth without losing oneself entirely?

Was it possible to reclaim those parts of ourselves lost in translation

> between digital pulses and real-world beats?

Is Your Smartphone Undermining Your Health?

While many of us are well-versed in the immediate discomforts from prolonged screen time, such as dry eyes and stiff necks, a more profound, insidious impact often goes unnoticed. This chapter delves into our digital habits' less obvious but profound health consequences. It's not just about the occasional headache or temporary eye strain; it's about understanding how our devices disrupt fundamental aspects of our well-being, including sleep and physical activity.

Our journey through this exploration begins with identifying **subtle yet significant physical effects** that stem from continuous device use. These aren't always as overt as a sore back or tired eyes. For instance, how often do we consider our breathing patterns or even slight changes in our stress levels when deep into our devices? These subtle shifts play a critical role in our overall health ecosystem.

Next, we address how technology affects our natural sleep cycles. The blue light from screens is well-known for reducing melatonin production, a hormone essential for regulating sleep. However, the impact extends beyond just this biochemical interaction. The nature of content consumption—whether it's late-night scrolling through social media or binge-watching TV shows—also plays a pivotal role in **disrupting our**

sleep patterns. This disruption is not merely about losing an hour or two of rest but disturbing sleep quality and restorative value.

Furthermore, the modern lifestyle encouraged by excessive screen time inherently promotes **sedentarism**. The convenience of having everything just a click away reduces the need to move, which has long-term effects on physical health, including increased risks for chronic diseases like diabetes and heart disease. Here, we'll explore how intertwined our digital behaviors are with physical inactivity and what it means for our health.

This discussion naturally leads us to examine the long-term consequences of these behaviors. Chronic conditions don't develop overnight but emerge from sustained habits and routines. In assessing these impacts, it becomes clear why moderating our screen time isn't just advisable but necessary for maintaining long-term health.

To navigate these challenges, we will outline practical strategies and actionable steps to help reduce screen time and mitigate its health impacts. These solutions are designed to be achievable and valuable, from setting up tech-free zones in your home to incorporating specific 'screen breaks' throughout your day.

As we progress through this chapter, remember that awareness is the first step towards change. By understanding the full scope of how our devices affect us physically, we can make more informed choices that support our digital well-being and overall health.

In essence, this exploration is not about demonizing technology but about fostering a healthier relationship with it. It's about taking back control and ensuring that our devices enhance rather than dictate the quality of our lives.

Prolonged Device Use and Physical Health

When we think about the effects of too much screen time, common complaints like sore eyes or a stiff neck might spring to mind. However, the impact extends further, infiltrating more aspects of our physical health than we might initially realize. Prolonged device usage often leads to subtle yet significant changes in our body, affecting our overall well-being in ways we might not immediately notice.

Imagine your body as a complex machine that operates best when active and engaged in various tasks. When we sit glued to our screens, it's akin to using this machine for just one function, over and over. This limited use can lead to wear and tear in certain parts while others remain underused, leading to a range of physical issues beyond the obvious.

Research indicates that excessive screen time can lead to poor posture, which can cause chronic back pain and muscle weakness. This is not just about a sore back or stiff shoulders; it is about a gradual decline in the health of our musculoskeletal system. Over time, this can decrease our quality of life and increase the risk of injuries.

Beyond the bones and muscles, our internal systems are also at stake. For example, prolonged sitting can affect blood circulation and increase the risk of cardiovascular diseases. It's not just about stiff or achy joints—it's about the long-term health risks that slowly creep up on us.

Prolonged device use can subtly undermine our physical health in ways we might not immediately connect to our screen habits.

Sleep Disruption and Sedentary Lifestyles

Have you ever found yourself scrolling through your phone late at night, even though you know it's past bedtime? This habit is more harmful than it seems. The blue light emitted by screens can disrupt the natural production of melatonin, the hormone responsible for regulating sleep. This disruption can lead to difficulty falling asleep, poor sleep quality, and various health issues, from mood swings to decreased cognitive function.

Why do we keep our eyes glued to the screen when we know it's time to rest? This rhetorical question highlights digital devices' grip on our routines and bodies. It's not just the immediate allure of content but how these habits insidiously impact our natural sleep cycles.

A sedentary lifestyle, encouraged by long hours of screen time, is another silent culprit. It's like settling into a comfortable couch that you never want to leave—except this comfort can lead to serious health issues such as obesity, type 2 diabetes, and other metabolic syndromes.

Consider this: if excessive screen time is the thief of the night, stealing our wholesome sleep, then sedentary behavior is the chain that keeps us tied down, preventing us from moving freely in the world of physical health.

To fully comprehend the impact, research has indicated that disrupted sleep patterns and sedentary behavior can reduce life expectancy and increase the risk of chronic diseases. These findings are a significant, hidden cost of our modern, plugged-in lifestyle.

Could reevaluating our screen time be the key to better health and longer life?

Long-term Health Consequences

Continual exposure to devices isn't just a risk factor for immediate discomfort or sleepless nights; it sets the stage for more severe health complications down the road. Chronic conditions like heart disease, diabetes, and deep vein thrombosis can all be associated with the lifestyle that comes with excessive device use.

Consider the analogy of a car. If a vehicle is driven too hard and poorly maintained with regular breaks and servicing, it's likely to break down earlier. Similarly, our bodies need downtime away from screens to sustain mental and physical health.

The link between screen time and mental health is also significant, with studies indicating a correlation between excessive screen use and increased rates of depression and anxiety. It's not just about the physical symptoms but the overall quality of life.

Taking steps to reduce screen time can be seen as preventive healthcare. It's about controlling the "inputs" we allow into our lives and ensuring they contribute positively to our health and well-being.

The long-term health consequences of continuous device dependence highlight the need for moderated technology use. Understanding these risks can help us proactively mitigate them and improve our health.

As we wrap up our exploration of the less obvious but significant physical effects of prolonged device usage, it is crucial to recognize that the impact extends far beyond immediate discomforts like backaches or eye strain. **Disrupted sleep patterns** and increased **sedentary behavior** are subtle yet powerful ways our health is compromised, often manifesting quietly over time. These conditions deteriorate our physical well-being and our ability to function optimally in our daily lives.

Understanding these impacts helps us appreciate the necessity of implementing sustainable strategies to moderate our device usage. It's not merely about alleviating discomfort but fostering a lifestyle supporting long-term health and vitality. The evidence reviewed underscores the importance of being proactive about digital habits, mainly their influence on our health landscape.

Adopting practical and manageable changes is essential to effectively navigating these challenges. Possible solutions include implementing stricter boundaries around device use, particularly during the evening, to enhance sleep quality or incorporating regular breaks and physical activity into daily routines to counteract the effects of sedentary behavior.

By committing to these adjustments, we enhance our immediate quality of life and invest in our long-term health, ensuring that we remain vibrant and active for years. As we move forward, let us carry with us the understanding that managing our interaction with digital devices is not just about preventing discomfort but about actively promoting a healthier, more balanced life.

Chapter 3: The High Price of Lost Time

Can We Ever Truly Disconnect?

Ella sat by the window of her small, sunlit kitchen, the gentle hum of the city drifting in with the morning breeze. She held a steaming cup of coffee close to her chest, feeling the warmth seep into her palms. Across the room, her phone buzzed relentlessly on the wooden table, starkly contrasting to the tranquil morning. She fixed her gaze on it, feeling tempted, but firmly resisted; today, she aimed to be different.

Outside, children laughed as they chased each other around the park. Ella watched them momentarily, their joy untethered by screens or digital beeps. It reminded her of her childhood, filled with scraped knees and sunset curfews rather than pixels and notifications. She sighed, remembering how simple happiness seemed back then.

The phone buzzed again, more insistent this time. It was probably her boss or another email demanding immediate attention. Lately, every ding felt like a chain yanking her back from the brink of freedom she desperately craved. The cost of her screen time wasn't just about missed emails or delayed responses; it was also about lost afternoons at parks, unread books collecting dust on her shelves, and unmade memories with friends who had slowly stopped calling.

She placed her cup down and walked over to silence the device. Finally, as she pressed down on its cool surface, she paused. There was something deeply unsettling about how dependent she had become on this sleek piece of technology, which dictated how she worked and lived.

With a deep breath drawn from resolve rather than resignation, Ella grabbed a light jacket and stepped out into the day's embrace without her phone. The air outside tasted different without the metallic tang of urgency that usually accompanied it from constant notifications and calls.

As she walked towards the park where children's laughter still filled the air like music from another era—one less complicated and more physically present—she wondered about all she had missed while living behind screens. Each step felt like a small reclaiming of those lost opportunities for personal growth and happiness that devices subtly stole away.

Is reclaiming our lives from digital distractions genuinely possible in this connected age?

Is Your Screen Stealing Your Life's True Joy?

As we navigate the digital age, our screens have transformed from convenience tools to *masters of time*. This transformation raises a pivotal question: what is the actual cost of our digital engagements? Understanding and managing screen time has never been more crucial in an era where every minute is precious.

The Silent Thief: Screen Time

Often, it's not the significant, noticeable disruptions that impact our lives the most; instead, it's the cumulative effect of many small ones. Excessive screen time quietly but consistently competes with opportunities for **personal growth** and maintaining **meaningful relationships**. Every hour spent scrolling through social media or binge-watching a series could be better spent learning a new skill, reading a thought-provoking book, or enjoying a heart-to-heart conversation with someone important.

Missed Connections and Opportunities

Reflect on your last week: how many times did you choose your device over direct interaction with others? Each choice might seem insignificant, but collectively, they represent a substantial loss in deepening relationships and personal experiences. This chapter delves into individual stories and reflections that highlight these missed opportunities. It's about recognizing moments when choosing the digital world contributed to a sense of loss or disconnection in our real lives.

Reclaiming Time for Joy

How do we then begin to reclaim these lost moments? It starts with awareness and continues with actionable strategies. The shift from passive consumption to active engagement in life requires courage and practical steps. This chapter will inspire and equip you with strategic ways to transform your screen time into time spent on more fulfilling activities. Whether it's through setting screen time limits or substituting phone usage with engaging in hobbies, these strategies are designed to restore balance and enrich your daily life.

The essence of this discourse isn't to demonize technology but to promote a balanced approach where technology serves as a tool rather than a diversion. The aim is to foster environments where individuals can thrive in both digital and physical realms without sacrificing one for the other.

In sum, by recognizing the profound impact that unchecked screen time can have on our lives, we can begin taking deliberate steps toward managing and optimizing our time for greater satisfaction and well-being. Let's explore how we can better navigate our days to enhance personal fulfillment and nurture the relationships that make life worth living.

Analyzing the Competition Between Device Usage and Personal Growth

Every hour staring at a screen deters you from cultivating relationships or pursuing personal growth. The stark reality is that our devices steal our time and potential for more enriching experiences. This constant connectivity means missed opportunities for deep conversations with loved ones or time spent on hobbies that relax and fulfill us.

Imagine your day as a pie chart, each slice representing an activity. How large is the slice for digital consumption? This slice is disproportionately large for many, squeezing out smaller pieces representing activities vital for personal development.

Research shows that the average adult spends over 11 hours interacting with social media daily. This statistic is alarming when considering how much time could be utilized learning new skills, nurturing relationships, or simply resting. The impact is tangible; relationships suffer when individuals prioritize screen time over face-to-face interactions.

In a metaphorical sense, excessive device use is like pouring water into a bucket full of holes. No matter how much water you add, the bucket never fills. Similarly, no matter how much time we devote to our screens, it never truly satisfies our deeper needs for personal connection and growth.

Devices compete with life's enriching experiences, often affecting personal and relationship connections.

Reflecting on Missed Opportunities

How often have you postponed a coffee date to scroll through social media or choose a night of binge-watching over an evening walk? These decisions might seem small now, but they accumulate, significantly impacting our quality of life.

Missed opportunities are like forgotten dreams; they only seem significant once we tally them at the end of a year or a decade. The hours spent on devices could have been redirected to creating memories with loved ones, picking up a new hobby, or traveling.

It's not just about the time lost; it's about the experiences and connections that never happen. Each hour on a device is a missed opportunity to laugh with a friend, learn a new instrument, or finish a book. These are the moments that enrich our lives and expand our horizons.

Remember the last time you realized how quickly time had passed while you were online? This is a common experience where "just five minutes" turns into an hour. Reflecting on what might have been accomplished in that lost time is essential.

Imagine your life as a book, where each day is a page. Are you filling your pages with meaningful content or with forgettable filler? It's a question worth pondering.

What might your life look like if you reclaimed all those lost hours from your devices?

Practical Repurposing of Screen Time

The first step in our model identification involves tracking and acknowledging the extent of our screen time. By using apps to monitor usage, we can get a clear picture of how much of our day is devoted to digital devices. This awareness is the first step towards change.

Assessment

Next is assessment. Here, we evaluate the emotional and relational impact of our screen time. Tools like journaling or mood tracking can help us understand how device use affects our well-being and relationships. Are we happier after an hour on social media, or does it leave us empty?

Repurposing

Finally, repurposing our time means making conscious decisions to replace some of our screen time with more fulfilling activities and starting small with options like setting aside time for hobbies, exercise, or socializing in person. It involves consuming digital content mindfully, much like choosing a healthy diet over junk food.

By following this model—Identification, Assessment, Repurposing—we can transform how we engage with our devices and, by extension, enrich our lives.

By analyzing how devices compete with personal growth, reflecting on the opportunities we miss due to screen time, and actively repurposing our digital habits, we can reclaim time and the richness of life that comes with it.

As we reflect on the insights from this chapter, it becomes clear that our digital habits carry significant costs, not only in minutes and hours but in the quality and richness of our lives. **Device usage competes directly with the time we could invest in personal growth and nurturing relationships.** The awareness of what we miss when we choose screen time over life experiences is a crucial step toward making intentional changes.

This chapter has underscored the profound impact of excessive screen time on our opportunities for engagement and connection. Each moment spent absorbed in our devices is lost to potential interactions with loved ones or pursuits that enhance our well-being. Recognizing these missed opportunities encourages us to repurpose our time towards activities that fulfill and enrich us.

To move forward, consider practical ways to decrease screen time, integrating strategies like setting specific limits, choosing tech-free zones at home, or dedicating certain hours to undistracted family time or personal hobbies. The goal is to reclaim time, the quality of our interactions, and the joy of engaging fully with the world around us.

Embracing these changes requires commitment and consistency, but the rewards—enhanced relationships, personal growth, and increased well-being—are profoundly worth it. Let us be mindful of how we spend our time, ensuring that our digital habits support, rather than undermine, our life's richness and potential for happiness. Doing so makes us take meaningful steps toward a more balanced and fulfilling life.

Chapter 4: Captive to Connectivity: Battling FOMO

When the World Whispers Through a Screen

Ella sat by her small, sunlit kitchen window, a cup of coffee steaming gently beside her open laptop. The chirping of the birds outside formed a stark contrast to the silent buzz of notifications that illuminated her screen. She scrolled through her social media feed, each swipe revealing snapshots of lives she felt disconnected from—friends hiking in distant mountains, families gathering around lush dinner tables, colleagues at glamorous events she hadn't attended.

Her heart twisted slightly with each post, a cocktail of envy and relief swirling within. This fear of missing out, an uninvited guest in her mind, often whispered that life was happening elsewhere, without her. As she observed a robin hopping across the garden, its breast a vivid red against the green grass, Ella's thoughts drifted to last weekend when she had declined an invitation to go out with friends because she felt overwhelmed.

The soft click-clack of her fingers on the keyboard paused as she remembered their laughter in a video they had shared online—so carefree and vibrant. Her room seemed to close in around her; even the comforting warmth from her coffee cup couldn't dispel the chill of isolation that settled around her shoulders like a shawl.

Suddenly, her phone rang—a sharp trill sliced through the quiet morning air. It was Sarah, inviting Ella for a walk in the park later that day. The simplicity of the invitation brought a flicker of warmth to Ella's spirit. Yet even as she agreed, part of her mind calculated what posting about this outing might look like on social media. Would it show everyone that she, too, had moments worth sharing?

As Ella shut down her laptop and prepared for the day ahead, stepping into soft sneakers and tying stray hairs from her face, she pondered why these digital validations had become crucial to feeling valued and connected. The park awaited with its promise of fresh air and honest conversations—far removed from pixelated portrayals and edited captions.

Would this walk help untether Ella from this continuous need for online affirmation? Could stepping outside mean stepping away from those pervasive fears?

Are You Truly Free If Your Phone Controls Your Emotions?

In the age of smartphones and constant connectivity, a new psychological phenomenon has emerged with significant implications for our mental health: the Fear of Missing Out, commonly known as FOMO. This chapter delves into the emotional and psychological repercussions of this modern malaise, exploring how our digital habits tether us to a cycle of stress and anxiety that undermines our well-being.

The prevalence of social media and instant communications means we are constantly connected to the triggers that cause FOMO. This continuous engagement demands partial attention, where the focus remains divided between physical and digital tasks. The result is a diminished presence in either sphere and a pervasive tension fed by the worry that something better is happening elsewhere.

Understanding the Psychological Underpinnings of FOMO

At its core, FOMO is not just about envy or superficial jealousy; it's a deeply rooted emotional response tied to our primal needs for belonging and esteem. Seeing others experiencing events from which we are absent can trigger feelings of social exclusion or inferiority. These experiences are only heightened by the carefully curated portrayals on social media, where everyone else's life appears more fulfilling or exciting than our own.

Digital Connectivity: A Double-Edged Sword

While technology has undoubtedly brought unprecedented advantages, its impact on mental health can be debilitating. The compulsion to be online can lead to anxiety and depression, exacerbated by sleep disturbances due to late-night screen time and the blue light emitted by devices. Moreover, the comparison culture fostered by online platforms often leaves individuals feeling inadequate or dissatisfied with their real lives.

This chapter will explore practical strategies for reducing FOMO and transforming our interaction with digital devices to address its harmful effects. Establishing boundaries that prioritize real-world interactions and mindful engagement over digital consumption is imperative. Techniques such as scheduled "tech-free times" and mindful consumption practices can significantly alleviate the pressure exerted by FOMO.

Cultivating Healthier Mental Frameworks

Beyond practical steps, there is a profound need to develop healthier mental frameworks for our online presence. These steps involve nurturing a more balanced perspective on social media narratives and fostering self-compassion to counteract negative self-judgment spurred by online comparisons.

By understanding the triggers and manifestations of FOMO, individuals can begin to disentangle their self-worth from their online persona. This shift is crucial for mental well-being as it moves us away from external validations to internal satisfactions—where true contentment lies.

In summary, while our digital devices have become gateways to expansive networks and information, they also pose significant challenges to emotional stability. This chapter will help you understand these challenges and equip you with strategies to reclaim control over your emotional health in a hyper-connected world. It is possible to reshape how we interact with technology through conscious effort and informed approaches—to turn it from a master back into a tool.

Understanding the Psychological Basis and Impacts of FOMO

Fear of Missing Out, commonly known as FOMO, is a psychological phenomenon characterized by a pervasive apprehension that others might be having rewarding experiences from which one is absent. This fear is increasingly prevalent in an era where social media platforms continuously showcase highlights of others' lives.

Imagine standing outside a brightly lit window on a cold night, peering into a warm room filled with laughter and music. This is what FOMO feels like— a constant feeling of missing out on the warmth and joy everyone else seems to be experiencing. This analogy helps illustrate the emotional impact of FOMO, which can lead to feelings of sadness, anxiety, and lowered self-esteem.

Psychologically, FOMO is linked to aspects of cognitive behavior where individuals have a distorted perception of their social relationships and personal accomplishments. The endless stream of social updates exacerbates this by setting unrealistic benchmarks of happiness and success.

Research indicates that FOMO can lead to significant stress, as individuals feel compelled to be perpetually connected to digital devices to avoid missing out. This relentless need to be online can disrupt real-life interactions and personal contentment, creating a cycle of constant dissatisfaction.

FOMO deeply affects our mental health, pushing us towards a never-ending cycle of online engagement and real-life disconnection.

Exploring Strategies to Combat FOMO and Reduce Anxiety

To tackle FOMO, it is crucial to recognize its triggers. Social media platforms often serve as a primary catalyst with constant notifications and updates. Understanding that these platforms are designed to capture and monetize your attention can be the first step in regaining control.

One effective strategy is to consciously schedule 'digital detox' sessions where you allocate specific times to disconnect from all digital devices. This can help reduce the anxiety of constantly being online and foster a healthier relationship with digital technology.

Engaging in mindfulness practices can also be beneficial. Activities such as meditation, yoga, and deep-breathing exercises can increase one's presence in the moment, reducing the compulsive urge to check social media.

Another practical approach is to cultivate richer in-person connections. Investing time and energy in face-to-face interactions significantly decreases the dependency on digital validations.

Setting realistic expectations for oneself and acknowledging that it is impossible to participate in everything can also alleviate the pressure that FOMO exerts. Regarding meaningful experiences, it's about quality, not quantity.

Could exploring these strategies be the key to unlocking a more peaceful and present state of mind?

Establishing Healthier Mental Frameworks Around Social Media and Online Presence

Adopting a healthier perspective towards social media begins with self-awareness. Recognize the emotions that surface when you use social media: Are you browsing out of habit, or do you seek something specific? This awareness can reduce mindless scrolling and promote more intentional use of technology.

Consider social media as a garden. Just as a gardener nurtures the plants, pruning the unhealthy ones and watering the healthy ones, you should manage your digital interactions. Prune away the activities that drain your energy without providing value, and water the interactions that enrich your emotional well-being.

It's also helpful to challenge the authenticity of what is presented online. Reminding yourself that social media often represents a highly curated version of reality can help mitigate feelings of inadequacy or jealousy.

Lastly, redefine what success and happiness mean to you, independent of online narratives. Focusing on personal values and real-world experiences makes your self-esteem less tied to online validations.

By understanding the psychological impacts of FOMO, exploring practical strategies to combat it, and establishing healthier mental frameworks, we can significantly improve our emotional and psychological health.

In exploring the psychological underpinnings of the Fear of Missing Out, we've uncovered how this pervasive concern keeps individuals anchored to their devices and significantly impacts their emotional and mental well-being. The relentless pursuit of staying connected can lead to a perpetual state of anxiety and dissatisfaction, which is why addressing FOMO is crucial for anyone seeking to regain control over their digital habits.

Understanding the psychological basis of FOMO has allowed us to recognize its deep-rooted causes and how it manipulates our emotions. This awareness is the first step toward countering its harmful effects. Acknowledging FOMO's triggers and emotional responses, individuals can detach their self-worth from their online presence and social media interactions.

Implementing **practical strategies to reduce digital anxiety** plays a pivotal role in combating this. Techniques such as setting specific times to check social media, using apps that limit screen time, and prioritizing face-to-face interactions can drastically reduce the feelings of urgency and anxiety that accompany FOMO. These strategies help manage time effectively and cultivate a more satisfying and meaningful offline life.

Furthermore, **establishing healthier mental frameworks around social media and online presence** is essential. It's vital to foster a mindset that values quality interactions over quantity and appreciates present experiences over online engagements. This shift in perspective can lead to more fulfilling relationships and a more balanced life.

Each of these steps supports the overarching goal of this discussion: to empower you to live a life that values real connections and experiences over digital ones. By understanding the psychological impacts of FOMO, actively reducing digital anxiety, and reshaping your mental approach to online engagement, you are equipped to navigate the digital world in a way that preserves your mental health and overall well-being.

As we move forward, remember that the journey towards digital wellness is personal and incremental. Each small step taken to understand and combat FOMO contributes significantly to regaining your autonomy over how you interact with technology. Armed with these insights and strategies, you are better equipped to lead a balanced digital life and ensure that your devices serve you rather than you serve them.

Chapter 5: Reboot Your Relationships: The Power of Digital Detox

Can Disconnecting Reconnect Us?

Liam stood by the window of his small sun-soaked living room, a steaming mug of coffee in hand, gazing out at the lively city street below. The chirping of morning birds mingled with the distant hum of traffic. He sipped slowly, the bitter warmth contrasting with the cold glass against his forehead. The digital world, with its ceaseless pings and glowing screens, lay forgotten on the counter behind him.

Days earlier, a conversation with his sister had planted doubt about his digital consumption. She spoke passionately about digital detoxes enhancing personal relationships and real-world engagement. Her words echoed in his mind as he watched an elderly couple sharing a newspaper on a nearby bench. Their easy silence spoke volumes.

Inside Liam's apartment, the phone buzzed insistently. He glanced back, hesitating. His thumb hovered over its sleek surface before he decided against it and turned away once more. The decision filled him with an unfamiliar blend of anxiety and liberation.

As he walked through the park later that morning, the grass beneath his feet felt unusually crisp, the air tasted fresher, and even the sun seemed to embrace him more warmly than usual. Children's laughter cascaded through the air as they chased each other around ancient oaks. Each step took him further from his electronic ties and deeper into a world teeming with life's simple joys.

He paused by a fountain, its water dancing in joyful arcs under sunlight. An older man sat feeding pigeons nearby; each crumb thrown met with eager flutters—a tiny battle waged over morsels of bread. Liam watched this gentle chaos and genuinely smiled for what felt like ages.

With every minute spent away from his devices, doubts crept alongside revelations—was it possible that all these mundane beauties had always been here? Had he been too absorbed in digital realms to notice them? What else had he missed?

As twilight approached and painted the sky in strokes of orange and purple, Liam sat on a bench facing westward where children once played but now headed home in tired yet contented troops. His phone remained untouched in his pocket; even as it vibrated faintly against his thigh, he felt no urge to retrieve it.

This simple resistance led to new connections—to himself, others around him, and nature's subtle rhythms.

Will stepping back from screens guide us toward rediscovering our surroundings and ourselves?

Is Your Digital Life Costing You Real Connections?

In today's hyperconnected world, the allure of screens is difficult to escape. Each notification ping or screen glow pulls us away from the richness of our real-world interactions, often more than we realize. This detachment from tangible life experiences is costing us dearly—particularly in the realm of personal relationships. Recognizing and addressing this digital interference is essential for nurturing healthier, more meaningful connections.

The Hidden Cost of Constant Connectivity

While technology has undeniably brought incredible benefits, its pervasiveness can impede our ability to engage in deep, fulfilling personal interactions. Regular **digital detoxes**—deliberate breaks from electronic devices—can help mitigate these effects. By setting aside our digital tools, we regain time and improve our capacity for empathy, attention, and genuine connection with others.

Planning Your Digital Detox Journey

Practical strategies for digital detox require thoughtful planning. It's not just about turning off devices but understanding the reasons behind it. Embarking on a digital detox requires more than good intentions; it demands a strategic approach and setting clear, personal goals for the detox. This may involve identifying specific times and contexts where disconnecting will yield the most significant benefits. Whether you start small by implementing gradual changes during meals with family, intimate moments with friends, or solitary times reserved for self-reflection, these periods, free from digital distractions, are crucial for revitalizing our relationships.

Consider your digital detox plan as a map. Similar to how a map helps you navigate unfamiliar territory, a well-organized plan enables you to navigate digital disconnection. This plan could involve having specific areas in your home where digital devices are not allowed or when all family members agree to put away their digital devices.

Initiating Effective Digital Detox Strategies

Executing this plan is crucial. It involves adhering to your set guidelines and preparing for potential challenges. For example, if you're used to ending your day by watching videos, consider replacing this habit with reading or meditating.

Engagement during a digital detox is vital. Communicate with your friends and family about your detox plan. Their support can make the transition smoother and more effective. Moreover, engaging others may inspire them to join you, creating a supportive community around healthier digital habits.

Observation plays a significant role. Pay attention to how your interactions change during the detox period. Are your conversations more thoughtful? Is your mind less cluttered? Observing these changes can motivate you to continue with these practices.

Reaping Relationship Rewards

Many find improvement in their interpersonal interactions and presence after implementing these strategies. Reclaiming time from our screens enhances our ability to listen actively and respond more thoughtfully—qualities essential for deepening relationships.

The effects extend beyond just feeling more connected to those around us; they also include a better understanding of non-verbal cues and a greater appreciation for face-to-face communication. The outcome? More robust and resilient connections that enrich every aspect of our lives.

Why This Matters

It's important to understand that the goal of a digital detox isn't merely to use technology less but to use it more effectively—ensuring that when we turn to our devices, it's with intention and purpose, not out of habit or compulsion. Balancing our online activities with offline engagements brings many benefits beyond mere social interactions; it enhances our mental wellbeing and overall quality of life.

Each step taken towards reducing screen time is a step towards reclaiming the narrative of your life—making it richer, fuller, and infinitely more connected. As you plan your journey towards digital minimalism, remember the power to change your relationship with technology lies squarely in your hands—and the right strategies can make all the difference.

With actionable advice rooted in proven strategies, this exploration into digital detoxification offers a path toward surviving in a digital age and thriving within it by fostering significant relationships.

Discovering the Benefits of Regular Digital Detoxes on Personal Relationships

The personal touch often gets lost in a world saturated with digital interactions. A digital detox, which involves stepping back from electronic devices, can help restore this personal touch. People often find that their relationships deepen when they disconnect from their screens. Research shows that face-to-face interactions can improve understanding among individuals and increase empathy.

Imagine your relationships as gardens. Just as a garden requires water, sunlight, and care to thrive, relationships need attention and direct interaction to grow. Continuous screen time acts like a shade, blocking the essential elements for these relationships to flourish. A digital detox acts as pruning, reducing the excess to let the sunlight in again.

Studies have shown that excessive use of digital devices can lead to miscommunications and misunderstandings. Face-to-face conversations, non-verbal cues, and emotional subtleties cannot be recreated entirely in digital communication. By reducing screen time, individuals often report feeling more connected and attuned to the needs and emotions of those around them.

Furthermore, digital detoxes can help re-establish boundaries that technology's constant availability has blurred. It's about quality over quantity. Engaging less frequently but more meaningfully can transform relationships from superficially connected to truly understanding each other.

Regular digital detoxes significantly enhance the quality of personal relationships by encouraging more meaningful and empathetic interactions.

How might your relationships transform if screens were no longer the center of your interactions?

Evaluating Improvements in Real-World Interactions and Presence After Detox

The REBOOT Framework: A Descriptive Model for Digital Detox

Planning

Setting achievable goals is fundamental in the planning phase. These include reducing screen time by half or designating specific hours as digital-free. This stage sets the intention and scope of your digital detox, providing clear objectives to strive towards.

Execution

Here, you put your plan into action. Ideas could involve turning off notifications, using apps to monitor screen time, or leaving devices in another room during meals. Discipline is vital in the execution phase, and the groundwork laid in the planning phase is tested.

Observation

Now, you observe the effects of your actions. Are you feeling more relaxed? Do your conversations with others feel more engaging? This phase is about noticing the changes in your daily life and interactions caused by reducing digital consumption.

Reflection

Finally, reflection allows you to look back on the detox period. What worked well? What didn't? How have your relationships improved? This is a critical phase for learning and deciding what habits to maintain in the future.

This framework emphasizes the cyclical nature of digital detoxing. It's not a one-time event but a continuous process of improvement. Each phase feeds into the next, creating a dynamic cycle of planning, executing, observing, and reflecting.

Following the REBOOT Framework, you can systematically enhance your real-world presence and interpersonal relationships, leading to a more fulfilling and engaged life.

As we navigate the complex world of constant digital connectivity, the insights from this chapter underscore the profound impact that a digital detox can have on personal relationships and real-world engagement. By intentionally disconnecting from our devices, we reclaim our time and rekindle the depth and quality of our interpersonal interactions.

Regular digital detoxes reveal the subtle yet significant benefits of stepping away from screens. Relationships flourish when given undivided attention, and conversations become more prosperous and meaningful. This dedicated, screen-free time fosters a deeper connection with those around us, enhancing our ability to communicate and empathize without the barrier of digital interference.

Planning and initiating effective digital detox strategies is not merely about reducing screen time; it's about *strategically reallocating* this time towards nurturing relationships and engaging in fulfilling real-world activities. Whether it's a scheduled evening each week without devices or specific zones in our homes where digital devices are not allowed, these deliberate actions set the stage for more present, attentive interactions.

Evaluating the improvements in our real-world interactions post-detox provides clear, tangible proof of the benefits. Increased presence leads to enhanced listening skills, more empathetic responses, and a greater appreciation for human expression's nuances—elements often lost in digital communication.

To integrate these practices into daily life effectively, consider setting realistic goals and involving those in your circle. Discussing intentions and setting mutual expectations can ease the transition and create a supportive environment for everyone involved.

Embracing these strategies enhances our relationships and improves our overall well-being. Disconnecting allows us to reconnect more meaningfully with the world around us, proving that sometimes, stepping back from technology is the best way to move forward in our relationships and lives.

Chapter 6: Discipline Through Scheduled Screen Time

Can Discipline in Digital Consumption Change a Life?

Elena stood by the window, her gaze drifting past the rain-speckled glass to the bustling street below. The rhythmic raindrops tapping against the pane seemed in sync with her scattered thoughts. Today, she had set herself a challenge: no reaching for her phone, no idle scrolling through endless notifications. Just this once, she wanted to prove that she could reclaim her time and focus.

Inside her modest living room, the clock ticked audibly, marking time in a way that felt more real than any digital alert. Elena remembered how, just weeks ago, every ping from her device would pull her from whatever moment she inhabited—stealing away chunks of her life one notification at a time. It had been an exhausting reflex that left her evenings blurred and her tasks half-finished.

As she turned from the window, her eyes fell on the stack of books on her coffee table—books she had promised herself to read but never found the time for. Today could be different; it should be different. With a deep breath, she picked up a novel, its spine creased and cover slightly faded from being carried around but seldom opened. The texture of the paper under her fingers felt grounding.

Her phone lay silent across the room. At times, it seemed to beckon with an almost audible call, but today, Elena's resolve was firm. She recalled reading about scheduled screen time and how it cultivated discipline and prioritization—a concept that seemed simple yet revolutionary enough to reshape one's daily existence.

The aroma of coffee filled the air as she settled into an armchair—the beans freshly ground and brewed in an old pot that had seen better days but still functioned with unyielding reliability. Each sip reminded her of life's simple pleasures, which often go unnoticed when overshadowed by digital demands.

As evening crept over the city and shadows lengthened across Elena's floorboards, a sense of accomplishment gently washed over her. Today had been different indeed; productive and peaceful in ways she hadn't felt in months. Could this experiment become a new way of life? Could it be as transformative for others as it was beginning to be for her?

What other areas could benefit from such deliberate pauses and disciplined approaches?

The Power of Scheduled Screen Time

In an era dominated by digital interactions, scheduling screen time emerges as a vital strategy for those seeking to regain control over their daily lives. This approach addresses the chronic distraction caused by our devices and promotes a disciplined, intentional use of technology. By defining specific times for engaging with digital screens, individuals can better manage their overall device usage, leading to enhanced focus and productivity.

Scheduled screen time is about restricting access and creating a structured environment where technology serves us without overwhelming our day-to-day experiences. In this context, it becomes essential to understand the significance of implementing digital limitations and its transformative impact on one's lifestyle.

Understanding the Need for a Screen Schedule

The first step in mastering scheduled screen time involves recognizing its necessity. Without boundaries, our devices often dictate our schedules and influence our behaviors more than we realize. Establishing a screen schedule empowers you to take back control and decide when and how you interact with your devices. This proactive approach is crucial for anyone looking to mitigate the subconscious habit of reaching for their phone or computer.

Tools to Facilitate Discipline

Implementing any new system requires the right tools and strategies. Practical applications and settings available on most devices can enforce the boundaries you set for yourself. Technology offers solutions, from app timers to do-not-disturb modes, helping us use it more responsibly. Exploring these tools assists in adhering to your designated screen times and makes the process manageable and effective.

Observing Changes in Productivity and Focus

The most compelling argument for scheduled screen time is its impact on personal efficiency and mental clarity. By limiting interruptions and designating tech-free periods, individuals often experience significant improvements in their ability to concentrate and complete tasks. This section will explore how disciplined screen use transforms day-to-day activities, enhancing professional output and personal satisfaction.

Scheduled screen time is more than just a technique—it's a lifestyle adjustment that fosters long-term benefits in both personal and professional realms. By learning about its importance, employing practical tools, and observing the positive changes it brings, users can achieve a more balanced relationship with their digital devices. This disciplined approach ensures that technology enhances rather than detracts from the quality of our lives, enabling us to live more fully in the present moment.

Learning Objective: Understanding the Importance of a Screen Schedule

In this digital age, we are constantly bombarded with notifications, messages, and alerts. It's easy to lose time when scrolling through social media or checking emails. This is where the importance of creating screen limitations comes into play. Schedule a plan that outlines specific times for using digital devices, which helps manage and moderate device usage effectively.

Imagine your day as a garden, where time is the soil, and your activities are the plants. Without proper planning, weeds (unnecessary screen time) can overrun your garden, stifling the growth of healthier, more productive activities. A screen schedule helps you allocate the right amount of soil to each plant, ensuring that your garden thrives by giving time to digital and non-digital activities.

Statistics show that people who use a screen schedule report better sleep patterns, improved personal relationships, and increased productivity. These results are because they are not constantly distracted by their devices and can focus more on the present moment. Moreover, by setting boundaries on screen time, individuals find it easier to engage in activities that enrich their lives, such as reading, sports, and spending time with loved ones.

Creating a digital schedule isn't just about reducing screen time; it's about optimizing your daily routine so that you can live a more balanced and fulfilling life. It encourages you to make conscious choices about your time, a crucial step towards developing healthier habits and improving overall wellbeing.

Creating a screen limitation schedule helps manage and moderate device usage, leading to a more balanced lifestyle.

Learning Objective: Implementing Tools for Scheduled Screen Time

Various practical tools can be employed to implement screen reduction effectively. One of the most straightforward tools is using built-in features on your smartphone, such as Screen Time on iOS or Digital Wellbeing on Android. These features allow you to set limits on app usage, schedule downtime, and get detailed reports on your screen habits.

However, more than technology alone is required. It's beneficial to combine these digital tools with physical reminders. For instance, placing a clock in your workspace can be a physical cue to remind you of your screen schedule, helping you maintain awareness of time spent on devices without constantly checking the phone.

For families, using a communal screen time calendar can be highly effective. This approach sets a good example for children and fosters a shared commitment to reducing screen time, making it easier to stick to the schedule. Each family member can have input on the schedule, thus ensuring that everyone's needs are considered.

Incorporating apps that block distracting sites during work hours can also enhance productivity. These tools help maintain focus on tasks without drifting towards social media or other digital distractions. The key is to use these tools as aids, not crutches, to develop your discipline.

Consider this analogy: If your day were a canvas, unscheduled screen use would be like splattered paint, chaotic and without form. Scheduled screen time, facilitated by these tools, is like painting with a defined outline, leading to a more transparent and deliberate composition.

Could implementing these tools be the brush you need to paint a more balanced daily routine?

Learning Objective: Observing Productivity and Focus Changes

Once a screen schedule is in place and tools are implemented to enforce it, the next step is observing the productivity and focus changes. Many individuals report a significant improvement in both areas, as they are less prone to distractions and can allocate their energy more efficiently throughout the day.

For instance, by limiting screen time in the morning, people often find they have more time for a fulfilling breakfast or a brisk morning walk, which sets a positive tone for the rest of the day. Similarly, by shutting down digital devices an hour before bedtime, individuals can engage in calming activities like reading or meditation, which promote better sleep.

This shift in routine is comparable to pruning a tree; cutting away the unnecessary branches (excessive screen time) allows the tree to focus its energy on growing stronger and healthier branches (productive activities).

After a few weeks of following a screen schedule, most individuals also notice a decrease in their stress levels, as they no longer feel overwhelmed by constant notifications or the pressure to be constantly "on." This newfound calm contributes to a more focused mindset, enabling deeper concentration and more efficient task completion.

By observing the changes in your productivity and focus, you can fine-tune your screen schedule for even better results.

Together, these strategies foster a disciplined approach to screen use, enhancing your ability to focus and be productive while maintaining a healthy relationship with your digital devices.

Scheduled screen time is more than just a method to curb our digital consumption; it is a transformative practice that fosters discipline and mindfulness in our interactions with technology. By establishing and adhering to a well-defined screen schedule, we reduce aimless device usage and reclaim the reins of our daily productivity and focus.

Step 1: Assess your current screen usage

Begin by observing your digital habits for a week. Record your time on each device and note what activities trigger excessive use. This self-awareness is crucial as it lays the groundwork for meaningful change.

Step 2: Set specific screen time goals

Once aware of your habits, set achievable goals for reduction. For instance, aim to reduce your daily screen time by 30 minutes. Specify how these minutes are distributed throughout the day, ensuring they align with your lifestyle and responsibilities.

Step 3: Create a schedule for your screen time

Integrate specific time blocks into your daily routine dedicated solely to screen use. Be strategic—allocate times that coincide with peak productivity for work-related tasks and ensure you set screen-free periods, particularly during meals or before bedtime.

Step 4: Use technology tools to enforce your screen schedule

Leverage apps and device features that help limit screen time. Employ app timers, activate Do Not Disturb modes, or use website blockers to minimize distractions. These tools are essential in maintaining the integrity of your schedule.

Step 5: Be mindful of your screen usage

During allotted screen times, remain present and intentional. Avoid multitasking and aim to make each session purposeful, whether completing a work project, connecting with family, or enjoying a film.

Step 6: Evaluate and adjust your screen schedule

Regularly review your screen usage against your set goals. Adapt your schedule as necessary to refine your digital habits further, ensuring they always align with your evolving personal and professional needs.

This step-by-step process structures your approach to reducing screen time and enhances engagement with the digital world. By following this guide, you are set up to experience a significant shift in how you manage and perceive screen use. The outcome? A balanced life where technology serves you, not the other way around.

Chapter 7: Creating Tech-Free Sanctuaries

Can Solitude in Silence Reconnect a Fractured Family?

Ellen's fingers hovered over the keyboard, still and hesitant. The glow from the laptop cast shadows across her face, mirroring the flickering doubts that danced in her mind. She had read somewhere—perhaps in one of those magazines that lay scattered like forgotten leaves on her coffee table—that creating tech-free zones within a home could stitch back the fraying seams of personal connection. Her eyes drifted from the screen to the clock, its ticks slicing through the silence of her study. It was late, yet the idea clung to her like the evening chill that seeped through her window.

The dining room downstairs was shrouded in darkness, except for the faint moonlight seeping through parted curtains. Arguments had unfolded like napkins at that sturdy oak table, and laughter had once spilled like wine. Could it become their sanctuary? A place where devices were banished, and only their voices filled the air? Ellen imagined her family there—not as distant ships passing in the night but as anchors securely dropped present in moments.

She rose and wandered to this potential sanctuary, her hands brushing against the back of a chair as if to confirm its reality. The wood felt cool under her touch, solid and unyielding. Memories fluttered around her—her son showing off his latest digital creation at dinner, her husband scrolling through endless emails. Each memory was a thread pulling tighter on her resolve.

Outside, a dog barked sharply, snapping Ellen back from her reverie. She pondered how conversations used to meander at meals before screens became their unwelcome guests. With each thought, she constructed mental notes on how they might reclaim these lost connections: board games dusted off from old shelves, books with spines cracked open as if awakening from a long slumber.

Would they resist? Would they embrace it? The uncertainty swirled around Ellen like autumn leaves caught in a gusty wind. But beneath it all lay a more profound fear—a whisper questioning whether these tech-free zones could truly heal what time and technology had torn apart.

As she stood there alone, with moonlight for company, Ellen considered tomorrow's dinner not just another meal but an offering—a test of familiar yet uncharted waters.

> Could silence speak louder than any notification tone and reconnect hearts around this old oak table?

Where Will Your Mind Wander Without Wi-Fi?

In an age where digital devices dominate our attention, carving out tech-free sanctuaries within our homes emerges as a crucial mental and relational health strategy. This chapter explores the profound benefits of establishing areas devoid of digital interference, focusing on enhancing personal connections and fostering mental well-being. Individuals can create environments conducive to relaxation and meaningful interactions by designating specific zones as tech-free.

The Imperative of Tech-Free Zones

The omnipresence of technology has reshaped our daily lives, often blurring the lines between work and leisure, public and private spheres. The need to establish boundaries has never been more apparent. Bedrooms, dining rooms, and even certain times of the day can transform into sanctuaries that shield us from the constant pings of digital communication. **Identifying critical areas** in our lives that can benefit from such boundaries is the first step toward reclaiming our mental space.

Strategies for Maintaining Mental Sanctuaries

Implementing effective strategies to maintain these tech-free zones is crucial. It isn't merely about restriction but cultivating habits promoting **enhanced mental well-being**. These strategies are foundational to building a healthier relationship with technology, involving physical changes like rearranging spaces to discourage device use or setting household rules that encourage face-to-face interactions during meals.

Observing Changes and Reaping Benefits

The impact of establishing tech-free zones extends beyond mere disconnection from gadgets; it enhances aspects of our lives we might have neglected. Improved **sleep quality**, more profound **personal reflections**, and strengthened **family relationships** are just a few of the benefits users might notice. Such improvements underscore the tangible positive outcomes of reducing screen time in favor of real-world interactions.

The transformative power of disconnecting allows us to engage more deeply with our surroundings and the people in them. As we delve deeper into this topic, we will explore practical ways to integrate these sanctuaries seamlessly into daily life. The aim is to set up these zones and sustain them as parts of a balanced lifestyle.

This chapter serves as a guide to recognizing the critical areas where technology can be left behind to improve our mental health and personal relationships. It underscores practical steps for implementation and highlights the positive shifts likely to occur from such changes. By fostering environments where technology does not permeate every aspect, we allow ourselves space to breathe, reflect, and connect—fundamental human needs often overshadowed by digital demands.

Through thoughtful examination and actionable advice, you will be equipped to establish these zones and appreciate their significance in a digitally saturated world. Each step forward in this journey adds a brick to the foundation of a more mindful, connected lifestyle free from the constant intrusion of digital notifications.

Identifying Tech-Free Zones

Certain areas in our homes and daily lives naturally lend themselves to being sanctuaries away from the digital buzz. The bedroom, for instance, is primarily for rest. Introducing a no-tech rule here can significantly enhance sleep quality and personal tranquility. Similarly, dining areas, where families gather to share meals, can be transformed into tech-free zones to foster meaningful conversations and stronger bonds with loved ones.

Imagine a garden without weeds where every flower has ample space to bloom; similarly, creating spaces without digital distractions allows every family member to flourish in their interpersonal relationships and personal growth. This analogy highlights the importance of nurturing our environments to foster natural interactions free from digital intrusions.

On the other hand, living rooms and home offices often blur the lines between digital necessity and overuse. Setting specific times when these areas are tech-free allows us to create a balanced environment accommodating relaxation and productivity. This approach reduces screen time and helps set clear boundaries that encourage healthier lifestyle habits.

Children's playrooms and bedrooms naturally offer opportunities to create tech-free zones. Encouraging traditional play, reading, and creative activities in these spaces allows children to develop cognitive and social skills more effectively without the constant pull of digital devices. Establishing these zones helps nurture a generation that can engage and entertain themselves beyond the digital world.

Recognizing and establishing specific areas as tech-free can profoundly benefit our mental and emotional well-being. **Tech-free zones are crucial for promoting healthier lifestyles and enhancing personal interactions.**

Strategies for Maintaining Tech-Free Zones

Establishing tech-free zones is the first step; maintaining these areas requires consistent effort and strategic planning. One effective method is using physical reminders, such as signs or decorations, that demarcate these zones and help reinforce the rules set for these spaces. This visual cue serves as a constant reminder for everyone to unplug and engage in more human-centric activities.

Another strategy involves establishing tech-free times, such as during mealtimes or specific hours in the evening when all family members agree to disconnect from digital devices. These strategies ensure compliance and build a routine everyone can easily follow, making the digital detox process part of daily life rather than an occasional effort.

Engaging in alternative activities that do not require technology is also crucial. For instance, board games, book reading sessions, or outdoor sports can replace screen time, providing fun and engaging ways to spend time together. These activities entertain and build skills and healthier interaction patterns among family members.

For those who find it challenging to disconnect, gradual changes can be more effective. Reducing screen time by increments, substituting digital activities with comparable non-digital ones, and using apps that track and limit device use can help ease the transition from a tech-heavy to a tech-light lifestyle.

Involving all family members in the planning and execution of these strategies ensures everyone understands the benefits and contributes to maintaining these zones. It transforms the effort into a collective endeavor where everyone has a role and responsibility.

Could these simple strategies be the keys to unlocking a more present, engaged, and balanced life?

Observing Improvements

Once tech-free zones are established and maintained, the benefits become increasingly apparent. One of the most immediate improvements is in sleep quality. With devices away, the mind relaxes better at bedtime, leading to deeper and more restful sleep. Reduced exposure to screens, especially before bed, decreases mental stimulation, which can significantly improve both sleep onset and quality.

Reflecting without interruptions allows for deeper personal insight. Tech-free zones provide the quiet for reflective thinking and meditation, leading to greater self-awareness and clarity. This mental space is crucial for personal development and emotional well-being.

Family relationships also see a marked improvement. Conversations become more meaningful with screens out of the picture during designated times and in specific zones. Each family member learns more about the others, strengthening bonds and building a foundation of mutual respect and understanding.

Imagine each family interaction as a thread in a larger tapestry. Tech-free zones strengthen these threads, weaving a more connected family unit. This simple yet powerful analogy underscores the transformative impact of reducing screen time on family dynamics.

We create a healthier, more connected lifestyle by identifying critical areas for tech-free zones, implementing effective strategies to maintain them, and observing the improvements in sleep, reflection, and family relationships.

As we reflect on the journey toward establishing tech-free sanctuaries, we must recognize these zones' profound impact on our mental well-being and personal connections. We create spaces that foster relaxation and meaningful interpersonal interactions by consciously minimizing digital distractions. The benefits, ranging from improved sleep quality to deeper family relationships and enhanced self-reflection, underscore the significance of our efforts.

Step 1: Identify tech-free zones in your life

Begin by assessing areas where technology can be paused. The bedroom, dining room, and family time are prime candidates. Focus on activities that thrive on undivided attention, like reading or engaging in conversations.

Step 2: Create boundaries and establish rules

Open discussions with those you share spaces with are crucial. Set clear, agreed-upon guidelines to ensure everyone understands the value and expectations of these tech-free zones.

Step 3: Remove or minimize tech-related triggers

Physically removing devices from these areas can significantly decrease the temptation to revert to old habits. Designate specific spots for device storage, like a charging station outside the bedroom or dining area.

Step 4: Substitute screen time with meaningful activities

Enrich these zones with alternatives that add value to your life. Whether it's a stack of books, board games, or art supplies, these tools replace screen time with creative and fulfilling experiences.

Step 5: Reinforce the tech-free zones consistently

Consistency is vital in maintaining these sanctuaries. Regular reminders and positive reinforcement can help sustain the commitment to these zones. Celebrate the small victories, like an engaging family meal without screens, reinforcing these efforts' purpose.

Step 6: Reflect on the impact of tech-free zones

Continuously evaluate how these changes affect your life. Note any positive outcomes or areas needing adjustment. This process ensures that the tech-free zones meet their intended purpose and adapt to changing circumstances.

By integrating these steps into our daily routines, we reclaim control from our digital devices and enhance our quality of life. Disconnecting is a powerful tool for reconnecting with what truly matters—our well-being, loved ones, and inner selves. Let us nurture these sanctuaries, embracing the peace and connection they bring.

Chapter 8: Mindful Interaction with Technology

Can an App Really Change How We Live?

Amelia sat on the park bench, her eyes flickering between the playground where her daughter laughed under the sun and the glowing screen of her smartphone. It was a bright autumn day; leaves danced in a symphony of gold and crimson around her, but her mind was elsewhere. This morning, she downloaded a new app that promised to monitor and control her screen time, offering insights into her digital habits.

She recalled last evening's conversation with her sister, who had casually remarked on how often Amelia's phone was in hand, even during family dinners. "It's just how things are," Amelia had responded, a defensive edge to her voice she hadn't intended. But later, alone in the quiet of night, she wondered if there was truth in those words that needed addressing.

As she swiped through the app's dashboard, statistics displayed in clean graphs told an uncomfortable story of hours spent scrolling through news feeds and responding to work emails at all hours. The numbers didn't lie; they painted a picture of distraction, which gnawed at her now more than ever as she watched her daughter play.

A soft breeze rustled through the trees, carrying the sound of children's laughter—a stark contrast to the silent digital alerts populating Amelia's phone screen. She set the device beside her on the bench and watched as a young boy offered her daughter a shovel to help build a sandcastle. The simple act of sharing, so pure and intentional, struck Amelia deeply.

She picked up the phone again, this time navigating to settings within the app that allowed for scheduling specific times for notifications—times when she wouldn't miss out on real-life happening right before her eyes. As she adjusted these settings, promising herself more presence in these fleeting moments, she felt an unfamiliar sense of control—a feeling both empowering and daunting.

Amelia knew it wouldn't be easy to change habits entrenched over the years. Still, today felt like a start—a small victory in an ongoing battle between habit and intentionality.

Could this small tool on her phone teach Amelia how to reclaim time and meaningful experiences lost to routine scrolling?

Harnessing Mindfulness to Master Your Digital Realm

In an era dominated by digital interactions, it becomes imperative to reassess our relationship with technology. While devices offer unparalleled conveniences, their omnipresence can lead to excessive screen time, inadvertently shaping our habits and behaviors. This chapter explores how mindfulness applications can be pivotal in transforming these interactions from habitual to intentional.

The Rise of Mindful Technology Use

The impact of technology on our daily lives is immense and cannot be overstated. From the moment we wake up, we are bombarded with notifications and digital updates until we go to bed. While beneficial in numerous ways, this constant connectivity can lead to digital fatigue and disconnection from real-world interactions. **Mindfulness applications** serve as a tool for monitoring and actively controlling our digital engagement, helping us gain insights into our usage patterns.

Intentionality Over Habituality

The shift from **habitual to intentional** use of devices is more than just a practice; it's a transformation in mindset. By employing mindfulness techniques through these applications, users are encouraged to make conscious choices about their screen time. The goal is to enhance personal productivity and improve overall well-being. The applications designed for this purpose do more than track time—they foster a deeper understanding of how digital interactions affect our mood and mental health.

Understanding the Impact

Most mindful interaction with technology involves an acute awareness of its impact on our daily lives. Recognizing the amount of time spent on various devices and applications can be eye-opening. It's not uncommon for individuals to underestimate their screen time, which is why these tools are essential in providing accurate data and feedback. This knowledge empowers users to make informed decisions about when and how they engage with their devices.

We reclaim control over our technological interactions by integrating mindfulness into our digital routines. Instead of allowing devices to dictate our day-to-day activities, we learn to use them as tools that serve our broader life goals. This chapter delves into practical strategies that aid in establishing these healthier boundaries and habits.

Practical Strategies for Mindful Use

As we progress through this discussion, specific strategies will be outlined that facilitate this transition towards more mindful technology use. These include setting clear goals for screen time, using technology intentionally for productive tasks, and incorporating regular digital detoxes into our routine.

This approach enhances our ability to focus and improves our relationships and personal well-being by freeing up time and mental space for what truly matters. It is about creating a balance where technology serves as a bridge rather than a barrier—a tool that enriches rather than dictates our lives.

We understand and optimize our digital interactions through the thoughtful integration of mindfulness techniques and applications. This chapter promises to equip you with the knowledge and tools to foster a healthier relationship with technology—a crucial step towards a balanced life in this digital age.

Integrate Mindfulness Applications to Monitor and Control Device Usage

Mindfulness applications are crucial in transforming how we interact with our devices. These apps, designed to monitor and limit screen time, are modern-day guardians of our digital intake. By providing real-time data on how long we spend on smartphones and computers, they help us become aware of our digital habits.

Imagine your device usage as water flowing from a tap. Without mindfulness apps, the tap often runs needlessly, wasting water. With these apps, it's as if someone reminds you to turn off the tap when you've used what you need, conserving your time and attention for other essential tasks.

These tools offer features like app usage reports, reminders to take breaks, and options to set daily limits. They act as trackers and coaches, encouraging us to make intentional choices about our digital engagement. For instance, seeing that you've spent three hours on social media might prompt you to reconsider and reallocate some of that time to reading or exercising.

Mindfulness apps also support the development of healthier habits by allowing users to schedule specific times for using certain apps. This way, you're not merely reacting to notifications or digital impulses but actively deciding when and how to engage with technology.

By integrating mindfulness applications, users gain control over their device usage, turning unconscious habits into deliberate actions.

Shift Device Usage from Habitual to Intentional with Mindful Practices

The transition from habitual to intentional device usage is beneficial and necessary in our constantly connected world. Habitual use often means reaching for our phones or laptops automatically without thinking about why we're doing so. Intentional use, however, requires a conscious decision, asking ourselves if this is how we want to spend our time.

Mindful practices prompt us to pause and reflect before interacting with our devices. Start by asking yourself simple questions like, "What is my intention behind using this device right now?" Such questions can disrupt the automatic nature of chronic use and foster a more mindful approach.

Integrating specific times for checking emails or social media can drastically reduce the scattergun approach to device use. Instead of allowing notifications to dictate your day, schedule brief periods where you attend to these tasks. This method ensures that technology serves you, not the other way around.

Visualize your daily routine as a garden. Habitual device use is like letting weeds grow wild, whereas intentional use is akin to tending your garden carefully, ensuring that only what you want to flourish does so. This analogy underscores the importance of mindful cultivation of our time and attention.

How can shifting to intentional device use improve your focus and productivity? This question invites us to explore the more profound benefits of mindfulness in our digital interactions.

Foster Awareness About Time Spent on Devices and Its Impact on Daily Life

Understanding the impact of our digital habits is the first step towards cultivating a healthier relationship with technology. By becoming mindful of how much time we spend on various devices, we can start to make informed decisions about our digital consumption.

Awareness is key. Just as you track your spending to manage your budget, tracking your screen time can help you manage your digital life. This realization often leads to a more balanced approach to technology that supports rather than undermines your well-being.

Consider a simple analogy: your device usage is like your diet. Just as eating without awareness can lead to poor health outcomes, unmonitored screen time can lead to digital overload, affecting your mental and physical health.

Analytical Framework for Mindful Technology Use

Trigger Analysis

Every habit starts with a trigger. By identifying what prompts you to pick up your phone or start browsing the internet, you can begin to control these cues. Triggers can be internal, like feelings of boredom or anxiety, or external, such as notifications from apps. Recognizing these triggers is the first step in transforming your digital habits.

Behavior Mapping

Once triggers are identified, the next step is to map out behaviors. Options include categorizing your screen activities into essential and non-essential. Essential activities include answering work emails or making important calls, whereas non-essential activities could be mindlessly scrolling through social media or binge-watching videos.

Reward Evaluation

Finally, evaluate what rewards you gain from your screen usage. Are they contributing to your goals and values? If not, it's time to find alternative activities that provide more meaningful rewards, such as reading a book or spending time with loved ones.

This framework helps you understand and modify your digital habits and encourages a more intentional and rewarding engagement with technology. Over time, this model can significantly transform how you interact with your devices, making your digital life more purposeful and less intrusive.

By integrating mindfulness apps, shifting to intentional use, and fostering awareness of our digital habits, we can reclaim control over our device usage and enhance our overall quality of life.

Embracing Mindfulness in Digital Engagement

In an era dominated by screens, **transforming our interaction with technology through mindfulness** is beneficial and essential. By integrating mindfulness applications that monitor and control device usage, individuals gain a **powerful tool** for self-awareness. These applications are more than just trackers—they are a gateway to understanding our digital habits and reshaping them in a way that aligns with our deeper values and needs.

The shift from habitual to intentional device usage doesn't happen overnight. It requires commitment and consistent practice of mindful techniques. This chapter has highlighted how embedding mindfulness into our daily tech interactions can lead to more deliberate and purposeful use of our time online. By fostering an awareness of how much time we spend on our devices—and, more importantly, *how* we spend this time—we empower ourselves to make choices that enhance our well-being rather than detract from it.

Remember, the goal here is to create a balanced relationship with technology—using our devices as tools to aid us rather than as distractions that control us. The techniques discussed provide a **framework for achieving this balance**, helping us reclaim our focus and improve our quality of life.

As we move forward, let's carry the insights from this chapter into our everyday lives. Let's be mindful of our digital footprints and strive to ensure that each interaction with technology reflects our conscious choices. Doing so enhances our lives and sets a positive example for those around us.

Through mindful engagement with technology, we limit screen time and expand our capacity for presence, productivity, and personal growth. Let this be a guiding principle as we continue our journey toward a healthier digital lifestyle.

Chapter 9: Replacing Pixels with Purpose

Can Old Habits Forge New Paths?

In the quiet corner of a bustling city park, Thomas sat on an aged wooden bench, his gaze fixed on the small screen cradled between his hands. The sun dipped low, casting long shadows that danced across the pavement, and a gentle breeze stirred the leaves around him. Children's laughter echoed from the nearby playground, blending with the distant hum of traffic. Yet, none of this seemed to reach him; his world was confined to pixels and prompts.

Thomas had always been tethered to his devices, finding solace in virtual conversations and digital victories in video games. However, a nagging thought had recently begun to surface more frequently: was there more beyond this illuminated rectangle? Memories of childhood days spent climbing trees and biking until dusk flashed through his mind, starkly contrasting with his current passivity.

As he watched a group of kids abandon their game of tag to huddle around a tablet one of them carried, Thomas felt a twinge of responsibility. Was he contributing to this new norm where digital interaction eclipsed physical play? This question gnawed at him as he considered his role as an uncle to his younger sister's children. Could he lead by example and show them another way?

He imagined initiating weekend hikes or taking them to play soccer at this park instead of discussing video game strategies or watching movies. The idea brought a mix of excitement and doubt. Could he replace the ease and familiarity of screen time with the unpredictable nature of outdoor activities? Would they even enjoy it or see it as an unwelcome imposition?

His contemplation was interrupted by a stray soccer ball rolling to a stop at his feet. Looking up, he saw a young girl approaching timidly. "Sorry, mister," she said, her eyes flickering briefly towards his screen before meeting his gaze.

Thomas smiled and kicked the ball gently back to her. "No problem at all," he replied, feeling the subtle joy that this simple interaction brought — an exchange so real and present it made him pause.

As he watched her return to her friends, laughter pealing through the air again, Thomas felt a resolve forming. It was time for change, not just for himself but also for them.

Could stepping away from screens be the key to unlocking richer experiences for Thomas and those around him?

From Pixels to Purpose: Crafting a Healthier Reality

In an era where digital devices dominate our daily routines, the quest for meaningful and fulfilling alternatives to screen time has become crucial. This chapter delves into the transformative journey of replacing pixelated interactions with tangible experiences that enrich our lives and bolster our physical and emotional well-being. As we navigate through this digital detox, we focus on identifying activities that fulfill the needs previously met by technology, engaging more actively in physical and social realms, and evaluating the positive shifts in our health as we reduce our screen time.

Identifying Fulfilling Alternatives

The first step towards a successful digital detox involves pinpointing non-digital activities that resonate with technology's psychological or emotional benefits. Whether it's the sense of connection we seek from social media or the relaxation offered by video streaming services, a myriad of non-digital options can offer similar, if not greater, satisfaction. This exploration is not about forsaking technology entirely but about finding balance and enhancing the quality of our lives through diverse experiences.

Engaging in Physical and Social Activities

Physical and social engagements are pivotal in this journey. The tactile sensations of a physical book, the endorphins released during a group sport, or the warmth of face-to-face conversations can never be replicated by their digital counterparts. By reintroducing ourselves to these activities, we break the cycle of excessive screen use and rediscover aspects of life that technology might have overshadowed.

Assessing Health Improvements

Monitoring changes in our emotional and physical health is essential to understanding the impact of reduced screen time. This involves observing improvements in sleep quality, mood stability, and overall physical fitness. By documenting these changes, we reinforce the positive outcomes of our efforts and motivate ourselves to continue this path.

The transition from virtual chats to physical interactions or from online gaming to real-world sports does not merely represent a change in activities; it signifies a more profound transformation in lifestyle. As we embark on this chapter of our digital detox journey, we aim to equip you with practical strategies to facilitate this transition smoothly and sustainably.

Our goal is not just to inform but to empower you with knowledge and tools that will enable you to reclaim control over your digital habits and rediscover the joys of a life lived beyond the screen. Through practical examples and actionable advice, this chapter seeks to guide you toward a healthier, more connected existence free from the undue influence of digital devices.

In embracing these changes, we open ourselves to new opportunities for growth and connection that enhance our overall quality of life. Let us step forward into this journey with purpose and enthusiasm, ready to replace pixels with deeply fulfilling pursuits that nourish both body and soul.

Identifying Non-Digital Activities

The digital age has surrounded us with screens that cater to every aspect of our lives, from work and education to entertainment and socialization. Yet, the need for human interaction and physical activities remains intrinsic to our well-being. Identifying non-digital substitutes that fulfill these needs is essential. For instance, replacing evening social media scrolling with a walk or a book can enhance mental clarity and reduce stress.

Imagine your daily screen time as a garden. Each app or digital activity is like a fast-growing vine that, if not managed, can overshadow the vibrant flowers beneath – these are your real-world interactions and hobbies. Pruning back the vines by selecting specific times for technology use frees up space for other activities that nurture your overall health and creativity.

Many activities naturally fulfill the roles that digital devices have taken over. Board games, for instance, can replace online multiplayer video games, offering social interaction and strategic thinking. Similarly, attending live music or theater performances can replace streaming concerts and movies, providing a richer, more immersive experience.

A shift towards more traditional pastimes does not mean rejecting technology but rather a more balanced approach to its use. Hobbies such as gardening, painting, or writing in a journal can fulfill the creative and relaxation needs often sought through apps and websites.

The key is to find non-digital activities that resonate personally and fulfill the needs previously met by technology.

Engage More Actively in Physical and Social Activities

The urge to check notifications or browse endlessly can be overwhelming. However, engaging more actively in physical and social activities diverts attention from screens and boosts physical health and emotional well-being. For example, regular participation in sports can improve fitness, while group classes at local community centers can offer social connections without any digital interference.

Think of your energy as a battery. Physical and social activities can be like a charger. Just as a battery depletes with use and recharges with rest, your energy renews when you engage in non-digital activities. This renewed energy then positively impacts other areas of your life. Incorporating more physical activity into your daily routine doesn't require monumental changes; even minor adjustments can bring significant benefits. Elect for stairs over elevators or try short walks during work breaks. Each step away from the screen is a step towards healthier habits.

Social interactions also play a crucial role in our mental health. Regular face-to-face connections with friends and family can enhance feelings of belonging and happiness, reducing the isolation that often comes with excessive screen use.

Integrating community involvement—such as volunteering or attending local events—can foster a sense of purpose and connection to others, further enriching one's life and creating meaningful memories beyond the digital world.

Are you ready to recharge your life by plugging into the world around you instead of a device?

Assessing the Positive Changes

Reducing screen time has tangible benefits for both emotional and physical health. Studies have shown that decreased screen time can lead to better sleep, reduced eye strain, and lower levels of anxiety and depression. Physically, less time in front of screens often translates to more active time, which can help maintain a healthy weight, improve cardiovascular health, and increase energy levels.

Consider the transformation as similar to clearing a foggy window. With less digital interference, you can fully see life's details and experience emotions. This clarity enhances your ability to connect with others and engage more deeply in your physical surroundings.

Documenting these changes can be highly motivating. Keeping a journal of how you feel as you engage more with the world outside your screen can provide concrete proof of the benefits. This record serves as a personal reminder of your progress and an encouragement to continue.

The positive impacts extend beyond the individual to influence those around them. Spending less time on screens opens opportunities for richer interactions and shared experiences with others, fostering stronger relationships and a supportive community.

By engaging in physical and social activities, identifying fulfilling non-digital alternatives, and assessing the positive changes, we can effectively reclaim our lives from the screen.

Step-by-Step Guide to Replacing Screen Time with Meaningful Engagements

The journey towards reducing our dependence on digital devices is not just about cutting screen time; it's about replacing that time with activities that enrich our lives. The steps outlined below are designed to guide you through identifying your digital needs, finding fulfilling non-digital alternatives, and integrating these activities into your daily routine. This structured approach will help you achieve a balanced lifestyle, enhancing your physical and emotional well-being.

Step 1: Identify needs met by technology

Reflect on how and why you use technology. Is it for staying informed, connecting with others, entertainment, or productivity? List these activities and note why they are essential to you. This reflection is crucial as it sets the foundation for finding the best non-digital alternatives.

Step 2: Find non-digital alternatives

With your list of needs, brainstorm activities that can provide similar benefits without requiring a screen. For example, replace scrolling through social media with a coffee meeting with a friend or swap video gaming for team sports. Choose activities that resonate with your interests to ensure they are both enjoyable and sustainable.

Step 3: Create a list of replacement activities

Organize these activities into a list categorized by their social, intellectual, or physical needs. Detail each activity with information on how and when you can do it. This list will be your go-to whenever the urge to use technology strikes.

Step 4: Commit to engage in non-digital activities regularly

Set realistic goals for incorporating these activities into your life. Start with manageable time slots and gradually extend them as these engagements become a natural part of your routine. Consistency is key here.

Step 5: Evaluate the impact on your well-being

Monitor the changes in your lifestyle as you shift away from screens. Observe any improvements in mood, sleep quality, interpersonal relationships, and overall health. These positive changes are powerful motivators to keep going.

Step 6: Adjust and refine your non-digital activities

Finally, stay flexible in your approach by continuously refining your activity list. Drop activities that don't bring joy or fulfillment, and remain open to trying new ones. Keeping this process dynamic will help maintain your interest and commitment.

These steps reduce screen time and enhance your life with meaningful experiences that foster personal growth and well-being. Remember, every small change contributes to a more significant transformation in reclaiming your life from the digital world. Embrace this journey with openness and enthusiasm and enjoy the numerous benefits of living more authentically in the real world.

Chapter 10: Gradual Change for Lasting Success

Can Disconnecting from Screens Reconnect Us to Life?

In the soft glow of the morning, Tom navigated his kitchen with a familiarity that needed no light. The sun was yet to claim its throne in the sky, casting a dim blue across his small, cluttered apartment. Today was different. Today was the first day of his digital detox, a decision born from nights too long and sleep too scarce, eyes strained, and mind buzzing with the endless chatter of pixels.

He filled a glass with water, the sound crisp in the quiet of dawn. As he drank, he pondered last night's conversation with his sister, Maria. She had listened, her voice a soothing balm as she supported his plan to cut down screen time. "Start small," she had advised. "Let everyone know so they can help keep you accountable." He appreciated her words; they felt like a hand at his back amidst this self-imposed isolation from digital noise.

The park outside beckoned for his first morning walk—unaccompanied by his usual podcast playlist. Shoes laced and the door locked behind him, Tom stepped out into the brisk air that carried whispers of winter's approach. Leaves crunched underfoot, a natural symphony he rarely noticed over the din of streamed media. He felt an odd sensation—a mix of freedom and an unmoored feeling—as if he had stepped out of a well-worn map into uncharted territory.

As he walked, Tom's thoughts drifted to how much time he spent scrolling through news feeds before breakfast or watching late-night shows until sleep clawed its way in. The park was waking up; joggers nodded silent greetings, and dogs tugged at leashes with tails wagging like metronomes set to joy. He watched a young mother pause by a bench, her child laughing as he chased pigeons flapping in hasty retreat.

Would this work? Could simple changes like these bring him closer to peace or merely closer to boredom? His phone vibrated in his pocket—a reflex twitch urged him to look—but today, it stayed put away; today was for observation and living beyond the screen.

With each step on the dew-damp path, Tom felt that success might lie in reducing screen time and rediscovering what fills those spaces when screens darken. As birds chirped their indifferent songs above him and leaves rustled their timeless tales around him, one question lingered: Could stepping back from our screens be what we need to move forward?

From Incremental Changes to Profound Transformation

A gradual and thoughtful approach is not merely beneficial—it's essential in reclaiming our lives from the pervasive grip of digital screens. As we explore in this next-to-last chapter, the journey toward effective digital detoxification involves more than abrupt disconnections or stringent screen time limitations. Instead, it thrives on **incrementally adapting our habits**, surrounded by a supportive community that understands and champions our cause.

When we realize that our screen consumption has tipped into excess, the typical response is a drastic cutback, which can lead to withdrawal and eventual relapse. To counter this, a systematic reduction in screen time ensures that each step forward is sustainable. These pages will explore why **a gradual transition** is crucial for long-term success and how it can be implemented effectively.

Furthermore, the importance of having a support system cannot be overstated. Engaging friends, family, or even digital communities can provide the encouragement and accountability needed to navigate this transformation. We will examine strategies for building and maintaining these support networks, ensuring they are robust and responsive.

Reflecting on one's journey plays a pivotal role in any change process. It allows for adjusting strategies and setting future goals that resonate with one's evolving digital interaction preferences. You will be guided through effective reflection practices that help maintain a healthy balance between digital and real-world interactions.

Understanding Gradual Change

Understanding the importance of gradual change involves recognizing the inherent challenges and potential setbacks associated with altering deeply ingrained habits. This knowledge prepares you for the journey and equips you with patience and perseverance—essential for long-term success.

Building Your Support System

Remember that communication is vital while developing methods for **your support system**. Articulating your goals and needs clearly can significantly enhance the understanding and support of those around you. This chapter provides practical advice on leveraging existing relationships and forming new ones that foster a conducive environment for change.

Reflecting On Long-Term Success

Lastly, setting long-term goals requires a reflective approach, considering past successes and stumbling blocks. In this segment, we will outline methods for reflecting **on your digital detox journey**, ensuring that the insights gained propel you toward sustained success.

By integrating these elements into your strategy for reducing screen time, you stand a better chance at achieving your initial goals and maintaining those achievements long-term. This comprehensive approach addresses the "how" and the "why," providing a deeper understanding and more potent motivation for pursuing a life in which digital tools are managed wisely rather than allowed to dictate terms.

This narrative doesn't just conclude our exploration but ties together various themes discussed throughout the book—highlighting how integrated efforts can revolutionize our interaction with technology, enhancing overall well-being without feeling disconnected from what matters most.

Understanding the Importance of Gradual Transition

A gradual transition is not just a strategy; it's necessary to reduce screen dependence. Abruptly cutting off your digital interactions can lead to withdrawal symptoms similar to those experienced in substance dependency; signs can include irritability, restlessness, and even depression. Gradual changes help mitigate these effects, making the process more manageable.

Think of your digital habit as a large, heavy blanket you're used to carrying. If you suddenly remove it, you'll feel cold and exposed. Instead, by peeling it away layer by layer, you can adjust to the new environment slowly but surely, which is less shocking to your system.

Research indicates that when individuals gradually reduce screen time, they are more likely to sustain these changes long-term. This approach allows the brain to adapt to the decreased dopamine levels (the 'feel-good' neurotransmitter often released in high amounts during screen use) and develop healthier habits.

Support from friends and family during this time is crucial. Communicating your intentions to them can help them understand your mood swings and provide the necessary support. Ideas include engaging in non-digital activities together or simply offering encouragement.

A gradual transition is essential for a sustainable reduction in screen time.

Developing a Support System

Building a support system is crucial in modifying and sustaining changes in your digital habits. Just as a tree relies on a sturdy root system to stay anchored and thrive, individuals benefit from a strong support network to maintain their resolve in reducing screen dependence.

It's helpful to share your goals with those close to you. When friends and family understand what you are trying to achieve, they can help hold you accountable. They can also participate in low or no-screen activities, providing a social substitute that discourages screen use.

Why Do You Need Others?

Consider this: a single stick is easily broken, but a bundle of sticks is strong. Similarly, changing a deeply ingrained habit like screen use alone is tough. But with others, the chances of success increase. They provide motivation and remind you of your goals when your resolve wanes.

A Harvard study underscores the importance of social support in making lifestyle changes. Participants who enlisted friends or family in their efforts were more successful than those who attempted change alone. Results showcasing the power of community in fostering lasting change.

Steps to Build Your Support System

1. **Identify Your Supporters**: Look for friends, family members, or colleagues who understand your goals and are willing to help.

2. **Communicate Clearly**: Make sure they know exactly what kind of support you need, whether they're joining you in activities or just listening.

3. **Set Regular Check-ins**: Schedule times to discuss your progress and challenges. Accountability keeps your support system engaged and informed.

The Power of Shared Goals

Engaging in group challenges can also be effective. Initiatives like "No Screen Sundays" or "Digital Detox Weekends" with others can build camaraderie and make the process enjoyable. This shared experience strengthens relationships and reinforces your commitment to reducing screen time.

Could having the right people around you be the key to a successful digital detox?

Reflecting on Your Journey

Reflecting on your journey towards a balanced digital life is vital. It lets you see how far you've come and plan where you want to go. This reflection should be honest and thorough, examining successes and setbacks.

Imagine your experience as a garden. Initially, progress may seem slow, as if you are merely planting seeds. Over time, with consistent care and effort, these small actions grow into substantial changes, much like seedlings growing into a lush garden.

Consistently tracking your screen time and noting how you feel physically and mentally can provide insights into what's working and what isn't. This data is invaluable as it guides your future efforts and helps set realistic goals.

Setting Long-Term Goals

Setting long-term goals is about understanding what a balanced digital life looks like for you. It's not about eliminating screens; it's about ensuring your use enhances rather than detracts from your quality of life.

A Practical Framework for Long-Term Planning

1. **Define What Balance Means for You**: Identify the role you want digital devices to play in your life.

2. **Set Measurable Goals**: These could be daily screen-free hours or specific times when digital devices are not to be used.

3. **Adjust Based on Reflection**: Use your reflections to tweak your approach and goals.

Reflecting on yo**ur journey and setting long-term goals are crucial to maintaining a balanced digital life. These goals should be informed by your ongoing reflections and supported by your social network, ensuring they are achievable and sustainable.**

Gradual Change for Lasting Success

Achieving a balanced digital life is not an overnight endeavor; it requires patience, support, and dedication. The journey from screen dependence must be approached carefully and in incremental steps. This approach eases the transition and ensures the changes are sustainable over the long term.

Understanding the importance of gradual transition is crucial. As we've explored, sudden withdrawals from digital usage can lead to stress and a quick relapse into old habits. Instead, setting small, achievable goals allows for manageable and less overwhelming adjustments. It's about making minor changes that collectively lead to significant life improvements.

Moreover, **developing a support system** is fundamental. Communicating your goals with friends and family not only garners support but also helps them understand your new boundaries and expectations involving screen use. This network becomes a source of encouragement and accountability, crucial for maintaining progress.

When reflecting on this journey, setting **long-term goals** that align with your values and lifestyle is essential. Reflection lets you see how far you've come and realign your actions as necessary. This continuous action, evaluation, and adjustment cycle is vital to indefinitely integrating healthier digital habits into your life.

Throughout this book, we have tackled the pervasive issue of screen dependency and its impacts on physical, mental, and social health. We've provided practical strategies not only for reducing screen time but also for enhancing overall well-being. You should feel equipped to make informed decisions about your digital consumption and to foster meaningful connections outside the digital realm.

Remember, the path to reducing digital overload is personal and unique to each individual. Embrace the journey with optimism and resilience, knowing that each step you take is a move towards a more engaged and fulfilling life. Let's carry forward the lessons learned and harmoniously balance our digital and real-world interactions.

Epilogue

Embracing a Brighter, Screen-Light Future

The Path Forward

Admittedly, every solution has its challenges. The strategies discussed are not a one-size-fits-all remedy and may require adaptation to fit different lifestyles and needs. Moreover, the rapid evolution of technology means staying adaptable and continuously seeking new ways to maintain balance.

Further exploration into how digital tools can enhance well-being without fostering dependency will be crucial. As we advance, keeping a pulse on emerging research will help us refine our approaches and discover even more effective ways to manage our digital lives.

A Call to Action

Now armed with knowledge and strategies, I urge you to apply what you've learned and become an advocate for digital wellness in your community. Share your experiences and successes with others and help foster environments that encourage healthy digital habits.

Remember, every moment spent engaged in life away from screens is invaluable. In these moments, memories are made, relationships strengthened, and life truly lived.

Let this book be a beginning rather than an end—a starting point from which you continue to explore, learn, and grow in your journey toward a balanced life.

Lasting Impressions

To leave you with a thought that encapsulates our shared journey toward digital mindfulness:

"Technology is a useful servant but a dangerous master." — Christian Lous Lange.

In this spirit, may you master your devices and not be mastered by them, finding richer connections in the world's beauty beyond the screen.

References

Wilson, E. O. (1998). Consilience: The Unity of Knowledge. New York: Knopf.

https://www.academia.edu/2547760/Consilience_The_Unity_of_Knowledge

Stand Up for Your Health: Navigating a Sedentary Workday.
https://mikesbalance.com/sedentary-workday/

Social Networking - SI410.
http://si410wiki.sites.uofmhosting.net/index.php/Social_Networking

The Teenage Guide to Digital Wellbeing | Tanya Goodin.
https://tanyagoodin.com/digital-detox-book/teenage-guide-to-digital-wellbeing/

Digital Detox: Reclaiming Your Mental Space as a Student - Routinery Blog. https://blog.routinery.app/digital-detox-reclaiming-your-mental-space-as-a-student-17065

The Impact of Digital Experiences on Gen Z Mental Health. https://www.cielotreatmentcenter.com/post/the-impact-of-digital-experiences-on-gen-z-mental-health

Digital Detox for Students: Embracing a Healthier Tech Life. https://nandbox.com/digital-detox-for-students-benefits/

Crafting a Lifestyle: Navigating Choices in the Modern World - CelebsHaunt. https://celebshaunt.com/crafting-a-lifestyle-navigating-choices-in-the-modern-world/

7 Steps to Planning Your Next Digital Detox - Goodnet. https://www.goodnet.org/articles/7-steps-to-planning-your-next-digital-detox

Anandpara G, Kharadi A, Vidja P, Chauhan Y, Mahajan S, Patel J. A Comprehensive Review on Digital Detox: A Newer Health and Wellness Trend in the Current Era. Cureus. 2024 Apr 22;16(4):e58719. doi: 10.7759/cureus.58719. PMID: 38779255; PMCID: PMC11109987. https://www.ncbi.nlm.nih.gov/pmc/articles/PMC11109987/

Vaillant, George E.; McArthur, Charles C.; Bock, Arlie, 2022, "Grant Study of Adult Development, 1938-2000", https://doi.org/10.7910/DVN/48WRX9, Harvard Dataverse, V4, UNF:6:FfCNPD1m9jk950Aomsriyg== [fileUNF]

NobelPrize.org: "Christian Lange – Nobel Lecture, December 13, 1921https://www.nobelprize.org/prizes/peace/1921/lange/lecture/#:~:text=Nobel%20Lecture*%2C%20 December%2013%2C%201921

www.ingramcontent.com/pod-product-compliance
Lightning Source LLC
Chambersburg PA
CBHW071101240526
45471CB00016B/2283